ANTARCTICA
HUMAN IMPACTS

GREG REID

Smart Apple Media

To Kathy, Steve, Sam and Mia.

Smart Apple Media
1980 Lookout Drive
North Mankato
Minnesota 56003

First published in 2005 by
MACMILLAN EDUCATION AUSTRALIA PTY LTD
627 Chapel Street, South Yarra, Australia 3141

Visit our website at www.macmillan.com.au

Associated companies and representatives throughout the world.

Library of Congress Cataloging-in-Publication Data
Reid, Greg, 1955-
    Human impacts / by Greg Reid.
    p. cm. – (Antarctica)
    ISBN 1-58340-763-4
    1. Ecology—Antarctica—Juvenile literature. 2. Antarctica—Environmental conditions—
    Juvenile literature. 3. Nature—Effect of human beings on –Antarctica—Juvenile literature.
    I. Title.
    QH84.2R453 2005
    577.5'86'09989—dc22

                                                    2005042587

Edited by Vanessa Lanaway
Text and cover design by Ivan Finnegan, iF Design
Maps by Laurie Whiddon, Map Illustrations
Photo research by Jes Senbergs

Printed in China

Acknowledgments
The author would like to thank the following people for their invaluable help: Angela Berry, Beryl Hansen, Louise Harris, Carmen Galvin, Janine Hanna, Sandra McMullan, Eileen Shuttleworth, Joanna Taylor, Cathryn Williams, Eunice Wong.

The author and the publisher are grateful to the following for permission to reproduce copyright material:

Front cover photographs: Satellite image of the continent of Antarctica, showing areas of thick ice and land but not the permanent ice shelves surrounding the continent, courtesy of Worldsat International/Science Photo Library.

Husky team (left) and tourist ship (right), courtesy of Colin Monteath/Auscape. Albatross (middle), courtesy of Science Photo Library.

Back cover photograph: Scientist tagging seal, courtesy of Dr Nick Gales/Lochman Transparencies.

AAD, p. 18; AAP, pp. 9, 17; Antarctica Picture Library, pp. 23, 27; Colin Monteath/Auscape, pp. 5, 6, 10, 14; D. Parer & E. Parer-Cook/Auscape, p. 4; Global Publishing, pp. 15, 26; Felicity Jenkins, p. 28; Macquarie Net, pp. 16, 21, 25; Reg Morgan, pp. 12, 30; NASA, p. 24; New Zealand Conservation Department, p. 29; Patricia Selkirk, p. 13; CSIRO/Simon Fraser/Science Photo Library, p. 22; Joanna Taylor, p. 11; British Antarctic Survey/Science Photo Library, p. 20.

Background and header images courtesy of www.istockphoto.com. Frozen Fact background image courtesy of NOAA.

Contents

GLOSSARY WORDS
When a word is printed in **bold**,
you can look up its meaning in
the Glossary on page 31.

Look for this symbol to find links
to more information online.

The Antarctic

The Antarctic is a pristine, icy wilderness.

The Antarctic consists of the frozen continent of Antarctica, the stormy Southern Ocean and the isolated **sub-Antarctic islands**. The region is the world's last great wilderness and contains unique landscapes, plants, and animals.

Antarctica is one of the harshest environments for life on Earth. It is an island continent that is mostly buried under snow and ice. Antarctica has a thick **ice sheet** and thousands of **valley glaciers**, floating **ice shelves**, ice cliffs, sea ice, and icebergs. Its isolation and cold climate protected it from discovery for many years.

The Antarctic is home to unique ecosystems which depend on the **fragile** environment for survival. Since Antarctic exploration began, humans have caused damage to the area and threatened wildlife. Today, the continent has become a unique place of international cooperation. Managing the Antarctic is a major issue for all countries, both now and in the future.

FROZEN FACT

UNiQUE CONTiNENT
Antarctica is a unique continent. It is the coldest, driest, iciest, and windiest continent on Earth. Antarctica has the world's largest ice sheet, valley glacier, and ice shelf.

Human impacts and issues

http://www.aad.gov.au/default.asp?casid=3436

http://www.coolantarctica.com/Antarctica%20fact%20file/science/human_impact_on_antarctica.htm

http://www-old.aad.gov.au/science/AntarcticResearch/HumanImpacts/default.asp

Humans have been in the Antarctic for around 200 years. In that time, three main issues have developed—exploration, resource use, and climate change around the world.

As humans have explored the region, the activities of scientists, tourists, and adventurers have disturbed plant and animal life and caused pollution. Humans have also introduced plants and animals to the sub-Antarctic islands, which compete with **native species**.

Sealers, whalers, and the fishing industry have pushed many species, such as fur seals and Patagonian toothfish, to the edge of **extinction**. They have also disrupted the Southern Ocean ecosystems.

Climate change caused by **global warming** means that many ice shelves in coastal areas of Antarctica are melting. This affects animals such as Adèlie penguins that live in the sea ice. The impact of the ozone "hole" is unknown at present, but it may disrupt Southern Ocean ecosystems in the future.

Humans are now aware that the Antarctic needs to be protected. Human impacts have become issues for the management of the region.

Tourists and scientists can disturb the natural behavior of Antarctic animals.

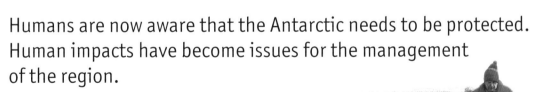

FROZEN FACT
BIO-PROSPECTING
Bio-prospecting is the search for useful chemicals in living things. Chemicals from Antarctic bacteria, algae, and yeast have been used to make medical drugs, cosmetics, and food products. There are no global agreements on bio-prospecting in the Antarctic.

Exploration

Antarctica's isolation and harsh, icy climate made it the last continent to be discovered and explored by humans. Although Antarctica has no indigenous or permanent population, humans have had serious impacts on the area.

Most early explorers in the Antarctic took animal, rock, and fossil samples and ate fish, seabirds, penguins, and seals. Explorers also introduced animals, such as ponies and huskies, for their expeditions, but the animals did not survive on their own.

Early sealers and whalers **endangered** many species of animals and disrupted natural food chains. Sealers and whalers also introduced animals such as deer and rabbits to the sub-Antarctic islands. These animals cause much environmental damage.

Recent exploration of the Antarctic by scientists, tourists, and adventurers has had a much greater impact. This is mainly because more people visit and they have modern machines. Scientific bases have been built and humans have polluted areas and disturbed plants and animals around the bases. There are 35 abandoned bases in the Antarctic, which need to be cleaned up to protect the wilderness.

http://www.mawsons-huts.com.au/history.html

Mawson's Hut

FROZEN **FACT**

HERITAGE HUTS

Some early Antarctic explorers' huts have been restored to preserve the human **heritage** and history of Antarctica. These include Shackleton's Hut at Cape Royds and Mawson's Hut at Cape Denison.

TERRITORIAL CLAIMS

Today, no nation owns Antarctica. However, before 1959, seven nations claimed territory in Antarctica. These claims were based on exploration and established bases.

Australia claimed the largest territory with 42 percent of the continent. Norway, France, New Zealand, Chile, Britain, and Argentina also claimed territory. Some territories overlapped and one area in West Antarctica was left unclaimed. It was the largest territory on Earth not claimed by a nation.

http://www.antdiv.gov.au/default.asp?casid=1295

http://www.antdiv.gov.au/default.asp?casid=6238

The United States and the former Soviet Union (now Russia), the world's greatest powers at the time, did not recognize these claims. They reserved the right to make territorial claims in Antarctica in the future. Several of the claims overlapped, creating the possibility of international conflict. In 1959, to avoid conflict in the Antarctic, the United States proposed the Antarctic Treaty, which all nations with territorial claims signed. This treaty set aside all territorial claims and made Antarctica a continent of peace and scientific research.

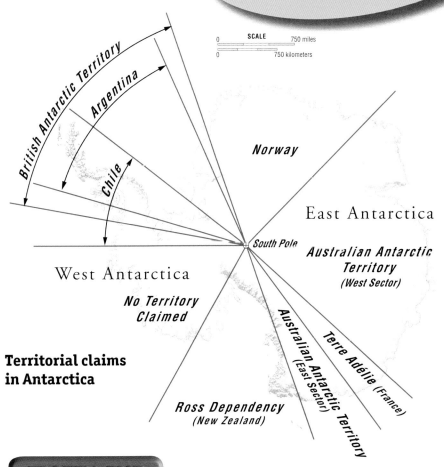

Territorial claims in Antarctica

FROZEN FACT

NAZI TERRITORY

In World War II, after Hitler invaded Norway, Germany took over Norwegian territory in Antarctica. To claim the territory, Hitler sent German flying boats to Antarctica to drop steel spikes with swastikas, Nazi German symbols, on top.

BASES AND SCIENTIFIC RESEARCH

Many nations have set up bases in the Antarctic. There are 74 permanent bases on Antarctica and 20 on the sub-Antarctic islands. During summer, the Antarctic is host to about 4,000 people, and about 1,500 people in winter. Each year, research ships bring around 1,000 scientists and crew.

Early 20th century bases were established for exploration and to enforce territorial claims. People on most of these early bases used Antarctic wildlife for food. Today, 18 nations have set up scientific research bases in the Antarctic and all food is shipped in from the outside world.

Most bases are found on rare ice-free areas, usually around the coast. These areas provide shipping access during summer for people from many nations. However, these areas are very fragile, and are easily damaged by humans.

Scientific research in the Antarctic provides valuable information about many things, including the unique Antarctic ecosystems and changes to the world's climate. However, humans affect the Antarctic just by being in such a fragile environment.

SCALE
0   750 miles
0   750 kilometers

General Belgrano II
(Argentina)

Mawson
(Australia)

Rothera
(U.K.)

A N T A R C T I C A

South Pole • Amundsen–Scott (U.S.)

• Vostok (Russian Federation)

• McMurdo (U.S.)

Dumont d'Urville
(France)

**Scientific bases in
the Antarctic**

FROZEN FACT

BOTTOM OF THE WORLD
Amundsen-Scott base at the South Pole was built in 1958 during the International Geophysical Year. It is named after the leaders of the first two expeditions to reach the South Pole.

IMPACTS OF BASES AND SCIENTIFIC RESEARCH

http://www.antdiv.gov.au/default.asp?casid=250

The affected area surrounding a base is called its ecological footprint. Some larger bases in Antarctica have researchers to assess the ways Antarctic bases and scientific research can impact the environment. These include:

* disruption to the local ecosystem caused by the construction of buildings, roads, and airstrips on fragile plant life and wildlife breeding sites

* noise and pollution from base generators, vehicles, planes, and helicopters

* fuel and chemical spills, toxic waste leaks, and soil contamination

* coastal and offshore pollution from supply ship accidents

* untreated sewage that is sometimes pumped into the sea where it pollutes marine life

* incinerated waste disposal that causes smoke pollution over a wide area

* discarded food scraps that make local wildlife dependent and cause deficiencies in their diet

* walking tracks and monuments that damage plants

* scientific research that may disturb plants and wildlife and increase the possibility of disease spreading to animal colonies

* abandoned bases and waste tips that cause environmental damage and spoil the wilderness values of the area.

In the past, some bases had open tips, while others dumped their waste into the sea. Today, all waste is shipped to its county of origin.

FROZEN FACT
DAMAGING RUNWAY
In 1983, the French built a gravel runway at Dumont d'Urville base. They blasted five islands that had colonies of Adèlie penguins and seabirds. A huge iceberg damaged the runway in 1984 and it has not been repaired.

9

Tourism

Tourists travel by ship, on sightseeing flights, or by land for unique adventures in the Antarctic wilderness. As tourist numbers have increased, so have the potential impacts on the Antarctic.

Most tourists visiting Antarctica come in large ships from South America.

SHIP-BASED TOURISM

Most ship-based tourism occurs in the Antarctic Peninsula and nearby islands because they have more ice-free areas. Each summer, more than 10,000 tourists visit the Antarctic by ship. Tourist attractions include historic huts, scenic beauty, and whales and other wildlife. Inflatable boats called Zodiacs are used to land tourists at special places to see wildlife colonies. Some ships offer helicopter flights.

SIGHTSEEING FLIGHTS

Regular flights over Antarctica began in 1977. Flights stopped in 1979 after a New Zealand aircraft crashed into Mount Erebus, killing all 257 people on board. Flights resumed from Australia in 1994. Today, aircraft fly at safe heights and at lower than normal speed to reduce noise and pollution levels.

LAND-BASED TOURISM

Antarctica has no land-based tourist facilities. The few land-based tourists are usually adventurers who come to mountain climb, ski, camp, and scuba dive.

FROZEN **FACT**

TOURIST SEASON
Ship-based tourists only visit Antarctica from mid-November to mid-March each year. After that time, the sea ice around the continent is too thick for the ships to get through.

IMPACTS OF TOURISM

http://www.coolantarctica.com/
Antarctica%20fact%20file/science/
threats_tourism.htm

A tour guide talks with tourists about human impacts in the Antarctic.

Tourists had a greater impact on the environment in the early years than they do today. There were no tourism regulations until the 1990s when the tourism industry realized that they were affecting the **pristine** wilderness of Antarctica.

Early tourism had many impacts on the Antarctic. Tourists trampled slow-growing moss beds and fragile soils. They left waste, disturbed wildlife, and took souvenirs from heritage buildings and fossil sites. Tourist ships released waste into the sea. Tourists came to see unspoiled wilderness, but instead, there saw signs of human impacts.

Today, Antarctic tourism is tightly controlled. Tourists are taught to keep safe distances from animals to avoid disturbing them. They are not allowed to bring food and water on land and they cannot use the bathroom or smoke. Tourist ships now take all their waste with them.

Special areas for tourism have been set aside so the impacts can be controlled. Antarctic tourism is growing at around 10 percent each year. This increase will need to be managed so the impacts of tourism continue to be controlled.

FROZEN FACT

TOURISM GUIDELINES

In 1991, the International Association of Antarctic Tour Operators (IAATO) established guidelines for operators and tourists to protect the environment. Today, all tourism in Antarctica largely follows these guidelines.

11

Pollution

Pollution in the Antarctic can come from human activities in the Antarctic and from outside the area.

❄ **Around bases:** Local pollution comes from bases and related human activities. Power generators and transport vehicles emit noise, heat, and fumes. Toxic waste and fuel leakage contaminate the soil and destroy **habitats**. Some bases burn their waste, and untreated sewage from some bases is pumped into the sea. In the past, waste was dumped at sea or in land tips.

❄ **In the Southern Ocean:** Regional pollution comes mainly from fishing activities in the Southern Ocean. Discarded fishing nets and lines, litter, and plastics are a serious threat to marine animals. Fuel spills from shipping accidents are also a major regional threat.

❄ **In the Antarctic:** Some pollution affects the whole of the Antarctic continent and the Southern Ocean. Global atmospheric and oceanic systems circulate small amounts of chemical pollutants from around the world to the area. Although this pollution comes from other areas, it is deposited in the Antarctic.

FROZEN **FACT**

NUCLEAR POWER REACTOR
McMurdo Station had a nuclear power reactor from 1961 to 1972. The reactor and more than 353,146 cubic feet (10,000 m³) of contaminated soil were shipped back to the U.S.

Power generators and transport vehicles at research bases cause local pollution.

IMPACTS OF POLLUTION

Pollution in the Antarctic threatens the pristine landscapes and ecosystems.

http://www.antdiv.gov.au/default.asp?casid=3122

http://www.coolantarctica.com/Antarctica%20fact%20file/science/threats_pollution.htm

❄ **Around bases:** Chemicals released by machinery and waste disposal poison the local environment, and plant and animal habitats. Untreated sewage pumped into the sea pollutes the coastal ecosystem, and burning waste causes air pollution.

❄ **In the Southern Ocean:** Oil spills at sea affect coastal and marine ecosystems. In 1989, an Argentinean Navy supply ship, the *Bahia Paraiso*, released over 26,000 gallons (100,000 l) of oil when it sank off the Antarctic Peninsula. Seabirds, seals, and shellfish died because the oil made it impossible for them to swim, fly, or find food. The oil may take more than 100 years to break down.

Some marine animals become entangled in debris in the ocean, and some swallow it. These materials also take a long time to break down.

This seal became entangled in debris and survived after it was freed.

❄ **In the Antarctic:** Chemical pollutants from around the world are passed through food chains by Antarctic plants and animals. Pollutants are also trapped in the ice and seabed, along with ash and other pollutants from natural events, such as volcanic eruptions.

FROZEN FACT
NON-POLLUTING ENERGY
Because Antarctica is the windiest continent on Earth, wind power is being tested as an alternative to burning **fossil fuels**. Australia's Mawson base was the first in Antarctica to install wind turbines.

Introduced species

Humans have introduced many species to the Antarctic, either deliberately or accidentally. Not all introduced species survive, but those that do can disrupt food chains, kill local species, and introduce disease.

Transport animals such as Manchurian ponies and huskies were introduced to Antarctica by explorers to help transport people and supplies. Sealers and whalers introduced animals on sub-Antarctic islands as emergency food.

In the early 1900s, British explorers Ernest Shackleton and Robert Falcon Scott brought Manchurian ponies on their expeditions to Antarctica. The ponies were unsuited to the extremely cold Antarctic climate and most of them died.

Husky teams were used to pull sleds in Antarctica for more than 100 years.

Huskies are thick-furred working dogs. From the late 1890s, they were used to pull **sleds** for most expeditions. After motorized vehicles such as Ski-Doos were introduced, huskies were mainly used for recreational trips. Huskies disturbed wildlife, polluted the environment, and were a possible disease threat to Antarctic ecosystems. They were removed from Antarctica in 1994 as part of an Antarctic Treaty agreement to remove introduced animals.

FROZEN FACT

MARINE HITCHHIKERS

Marine animals, such as shellfish, can hitch a ride on marine debris and move to the Antarctic from other areas. If they survive the freezing conditions, they can have a severe impact on Antarctic marine ecosystems.

IMPACTS ON SUB-ANTARCTIC ISLANDS

Introduced species disrupt sub-Antarctic island ecosystems in many ways. Once the animals are established, they are nearly impossible to get rid of. Introduced species often have no natural predators.

Invertebrates (animals without backbones) have been accidentally introduced to some islands in building materials. They eat plant material and compete with local invertebrate species.

http://www.abc.net.au/science/antarctica/ingrid/diaries/980824.htm

European starlings compete with native birds for food and nesting sites. After New Zealand wading birds, called wekas, were introduced to Macquarie Island, they wiped out the grey petrels by eating their eggs and chicks. On other sub-Antarctic islands, wekas steal eggs and chicks from seabirds, such as prions and petrels.

Rabbits overgraze plants and cause soil erosion on many islands. Cats and rats prey on nesting birds. On the Kerguelen Islands, cats threatened about 2,000 breeding pairs of Kerguelen terns with extinction. Rats have almost wiped out the South Georgia pipit, the world's most southerly songbird. On Campbell Island, south of New Zealand, Norway rats were endangering the native plants and animals, such as Campbell Island teal, until they were successfully removed in 2003.

The 2,700 reindeer on South Georgia have no predators and they damage the island's fragile plant life.

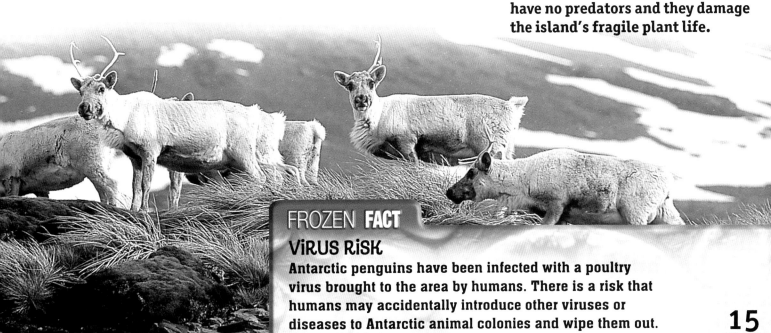

FROZEN **FACT**

ViRUS RiSK

Antarctic penguins have been infected with a poultry virus brought to the area by humans. There is a risk that humans may accidentally introduce other viruses or diseases to Antarctic animal colonies and wipe them out.

Sealing

When British explorer Captain James Cook reported that the Southern Ocean was filled with wildlife, sealers and whalers rushed to hunt these animals for profit.

http://www.antarcticconnection.com/antarctic/wildlife/seals/index.shtml

http://library.thinkquest.org/26442/html/human/hunt.html

At first, sealers hunted fur seals. Their dense, waterproof fur was in high demand for making gloves, hats, coats, and boots. Fur seal populations quickly declined on sub-Antarctic islands, forcing sealers to search for new areas. By the early 1900s, fur seals were almost extinct in the Antarctic.

Southern elephant seals became endangered after they were hunted for their blubber oil.

Sealers next turned to harvesting blubber seals for their oil, which was used as fuel for lamps, cooking, and industry. Even penguins were hunted for their oil when blubber seal numbers declined.

IMPACTS OF SEALING

Sealers hunted the Antarctic fur seal, the sub-Antarctic fur seal, the New Zealand fur seal, and the South American fur seal to near extinction. Some blubber seal species were also endangered by hunting. The removal of millions of seals upset the natural balance of the food chains in the Southern Ocean. Today, most seal species have recovered and none are endangered.

FROZEN FACT

SEAL AND PENGUIN TOLL
More than three million fur seals were killed for their skins. Over one million blubber seals were killed for their oil. Millions of penguins were also harvested for their oil.

Whaling

http://www.coolantarctica.
com/Antarctica%20fact%20file/
science/threats_fishing_
hunting.htm

Southern Ocean whales were hunted for their meat, **baleen**, and oil. Whalers moved from the larger species to smaller species as each species declined in number.

Early whalers targeted southern right whales, then humpback whales. In the 20th century, whalers turned their attention to open ocean species, such as blue and fin whales. New technologies, such as explosive harpoon heads, helped make this possible. When these larger species declined, whalers turned to sperm, sei, and even smaller minke whales.

A Greenpeace vessel protests against a dead minke whale being pulled into a Japanese factory ship.

Whaling was banned in 1982. However, the International Whaling Commission (IWC) still allows Japan, Iceland, and Norway to take a small number of minke whales each year for "scientific" research. The whale meat is sold for food.

IMPACTS OF WHALING

Today, southern right, humpback, blue, fin, sperm, and sei whales are still endangered. Whales are slow breeding and it takes a long time for populations to recover. Of the whaling targets, only minke whales are not endangered. The removal of most large whales has upset the natural balance of food chains in the Southern Ocean.

FROZEN FACT

WHALE TOLL

Around 1.3 million whales were harvested from the Southern Ocean. Less than 16 percent of the original whale population was left. Only one percent of the original blue whale population survived.

17

Fishing

Fishing and **krill** harvesting are the only ocean resources still being developed in the Antarctic. The larger fish species such as marbled rock cod, icefish, and toothfish are threatened with **overfishing** by humans.

The former Soviet Union (now Russia) began large-scale **trawling** for marbled rock cod and icefish in the late 1960s around South Georgia, an island off the east coast of South America. Fish catches soon declined so the fishing industry moved farther eastward around other sub-Antarctic islands, where the fish populations also quickly declined.

Antarctic fish are slow-growing and long-lived. They take a long time to breed and only produce a few eggs. Most Antarctic fish species live on the seabed and are smaller than one foot (30 cm). The slow life cycle of Antarctic fish means that it takes a long time for fish numbers to recover after an area has been harvested.

In the 1990s, **long-line fishing** for Patagonian and Antarctic toothfish became profitable. Illegal operators or pirate fishermen threaten the survival of the rare and valuable Patagonian toothfish around its sub-Antarctic island habitats.

Seven-foot (2 m) long Patagonian toothfish are endangered, but continue to be illegally caught.

FROZEN **FACT**

WHITE GOLD
Patagonian toothfish are also called Chilean sea bass. A major U.S. magazine listed it as the world's best eating fish. For poachers, its firm, white flesh is considered "white gold."

Many albatross species are threatened with extinction as a result of long-line fishing.

http://www.antdiv.gov.au/default.asp?casid=1539

http://www.bbc.co.uk/worldservice/sci_tech/highlights/010427_albatross.shtml

IMPACTS OF FISHING

The fishery around South Georgia collapsed after only a few years. Scientists estimate that only 10 percent of the original fish population survived the overfishing. After 30 years of protection, the fish stocks in the area have still not recovered. It will take many years for population numbers to rebuild. In the meantime, there is an imbalance in the Southern Ocean food chain.

Scientists predict that the Patagonian toothfish fishery will collapse by 2012 if illegal fishing continues. As toothfish are large predators, their removal from the food chain will create imbalances and unknown effects in the ocean ecosystems.

FISHING BYCATCH

Each year in the Antarctic, long-line baits kill more than 100,000 seabirds as unwanted **bycatch.** The seabirds drown after they swallow the baits meant for deep-sea fish. Many albatross species are endangered because of long-line fishing.

Trawling kills many smaller fish and other creatures as bycatch. It also damages other slow-growing life forms on the seabed and it may take a long time for the trawled areas to recover.

FROZEN **FACT**

TOOTHFISH PROTECTION
In 2003, an Australian fisheries vessel caught a Uruguayan ship with US$3.7 million worth of illegal Patagonian toothfish. Several nations have arrested people fishing illegally in Antarctic waters.

Krill fishery

Antarctic krill are small open-ocean crustaceans (shrimp-like creatures). A large variety of predators eat krill, making them central to the Southern Ocean ecosystem.

The former Soviet Union (now Russia) began krill harvesting in the 1960s. In 1982, over 492 million tons (500,000 t) were taken. Other nations that harvest krill include Japan, Ukraine, Argentina, Poland, and South Korea. Large factory ships process and freeze the catch at sea. There are likely to be increased pressures on the krill fishery in the future as global demand for krill products grows.

Krill harvesting will probably increase in the future as world demand for krill products increases.

http://www.doc.ic.ac.uk/~kpt/terraquest/va/ecology/ecology.html#A

http://news.nationalgeographic.com/news/2003/08/0805_030805_antarctic.html#main

IMPACTS ON KRILL FISHERY

Krill harvesting in the Antarctic is controlled to prevent overfishing and to ensure that there are enough krill to sustain the Southern Ocean ecosystem. Global warming is a potential threat to krill. A rise in sea temperatures may change the patterns of **phytoplankton** that krill feed on. High levels of ultraviolet (UV) radiation coming through the ozone "hole" also threaten krill. A collapse of krill numbers would affect all large animals in the Antarctic region.

FROZEN **FACT**

FOOD SOURCE
Humans harvest krill for food, bait, fishmeal, and stock feed. A decline in krill populations may cause huge problems in the food chain because so many species depend on krill in their diet.

Mining

Antarctica is believed to have many mineral deposits such as coal, iron ore, copper, gold, uranium, and platinum. Oil and natural gas may also exist in the continental shelf surrounding the continent. Only a small area has been explored and no detailed mineral surveys have been undertaken.

http://www.antdiv.gov.au/default.asp?casid=6561

http://www.coolantarctica.com/Antarctica%20fact%20file/science/threats_mining_oil.htm

IMPACTS OF MINING

Many Antarctic Treaty nations are concerned that large-scale, commercial mining in Antarctica might cause environmental damage. Mining would be difficult in such a fragile and remote area. Antarctica's isolation would mean high transportation costs, and the icy climate would make work very difficult. Most rocks are buried under moving ice, making them hard to access.

Scientific exploration and mineral research is allowed under the Madrid Protocol, but mining is banned until at least 2048.

In 1991, the Antarctic Treaty nations signed the **Madrid Protocol** to protect Antarctica from mining. The Protocol came into force in 1998 and bans mining in Antarctica for 50 years.

The mining ban will be reviewed in 2048. Mining may be allowed after that if it can be proved that the environment would be safe, and all nations who signed the Protocol agree. However, the difficulties involved may keep it from being profitable.

FROZEN FACT

COAL RESOURCES

Coal is found in two places in East Antarctica. The Prince Charles Mountains has good quality coal. Poorer quality coal is found in the Transantarctic Mountains.

21

Global warming

Antarctica is an ideal place to study global warming. It contains 90 percent of the world's ice and helps to regulate the Earth's climate.

Burning fossil fuels such as coal, oil, and natural gas releases greenhouse gases. These gases trap heat in the Earth's atmosphere and increase global air temperatures.

Scientists analyze ice cores from deep in the Antarctic ice sheet to find out about climate changes in the past.

There have been several natural cycles of ice ages and warmer periods in Earth's history. These historic cycles are all recorded like fossils in the million-year-old ice sheet of Antarctica. Scientists study pockets of air trapped in ancient Antarctic ice to record the Earth's past atmosphere. This helps them to understand what is happening at present.

Scientists are trying to figure out how global warming affects these natural warmer and colder cycles of the Earth. They measure the temperature of the atmosphere over Antarctica to look for changes. Scientists also study the Antarctic ice sheet, valley glaciers, and ice shelves. They look for changes in ice thickness, size, and speed of movement to see the effects of global warming.

FROZEN **FACT**

ANCIENT CLIMATE CLUES
Scientists in Germany are studying the world's oldest ice to help them understand climate change. The ice is up to 900,000 years old and from two miles (3.2 km) below the Antarctic ice sheet.

GLOBAL WARMING IN THE ANTARCTIC

Since the 1950s, the Antarctic Peninsula has warmed by 4.5°F (2.5°C), while the center of Antarctica has become colder. About half of the warming of the Antarctic Peninsula is due to global warming. The other half is caused by the Southern Ocean Vortex, a mass of swirling air driven by changes to the ozone "hole" every spring. It sucks warmer air from tropical areas and carries it farther south than normal.

http://www.doc.ic.ac.uk/~kpt/
terraquest/va/ecology/ecology.html

http://www.antarctica.ac.uk/About_
Antarctica/FAQs/faq_02.html

Global warming will cause greater snowfall on Antarctica due to increased water vapor in the air above the Southern Ocean. This will also thicken the ice sheet and valley glaciers, increase movement of ice, and create more icebergs. The ice shelves around the coast of Antarctica will melt faster than before.

IMPACT OF ANTARCTIC WARMING AROUND THE WORLD

The increase in ice sheet movement and numbers of icebergs could cause global sea levels to rise by three feet (1 m) this century. This will flood low-lying coastal areas and countries such as the Netherlands and the Maldives. Winters will be warmer and there will be many climatic changes.

Global warming will result in more Antarctic icebergs and an increase in sea levels.

FROZEN FACT

SHRINKING ICE SHELVES
The Larsen and Wordie ice shelves in the Antarctic Peninsula have greatly shrunk in size in recent years. This means that animals that depend on ice shelves, such as Weddell seals and Adélie penguins, lose their habitat.

The ozone "hole"

Every spring over the Antarctic, there is a thinning in the ozone layer of the atmosphere, 6–31 miles (10–50 km) above the Earth. This is called the ozone "hole."

The ozone layer prevents harmful ultraviolet (UV) radiation from the sun reaching the Earth's surface. In the late 1970s, British scientists first noticed damage to the ozone layer. The ozone "hole" was discovered in 1985.

Ozone levels are up to 70 percent less than normal in the ozone "hole." In September 2003, the "hole" was three times larger than the area of the United States.

People make chemicals such as chloro-fluoro-carbons (CFCs) and halons, which destroy ozone. These chemicals were used in air conditioners, aerosols, and refrigerators until 1987. CFCs and halons are no longer produced, but they still exist in some countries. Upper atmosphere winds carry the chemicals to the Antarctic where they remain in the atmosphere for decades.

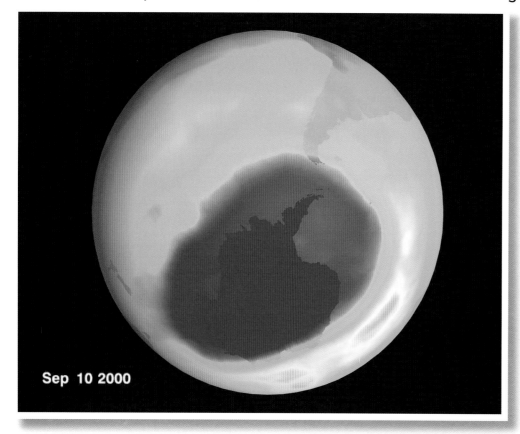

Sep 10 2000

The ozone "hole" over Antarctica

FROZEN **FACT**

HEALTH THREAT
Sometimes the ozone "hole" passes over southern Chile in South America. People are warned by the media about how UV radiation can damage their eyes and cause skin cancer.

Researchers release a balloon, called a radiosonde, carrying instruments to measure ozone.

IMPACTS OF THE OZONE "HOLE"

The ozone "hole" is one of the biggest human impacts on the Antarctic. Scientists say that the ozone "hole" will probably exist until at least 2050 when the damage might be repaired.

http://www.doc.ic.ac.uk/~kpt/terraquest/va/ecology/ecology.html

Scientists worry that global warming might reduce the recovery of the ozone layer. The combination of the ozone "hole" and global warming is making coastal areas of the Antarctic warmer and the inland areas colder. This will cause Antarctic ice to melt faster, raising sea levels.

Increased UV radiation may harm phytoplankton and the **larvae** of shrimps and fish. If phytoplankton is reduced, this will result in fewer krill, which would have huge impacts on Southern Ocean food chains. One species of Antarctic phytoplankton produces chemicals that help protect it from UV radiation. Unfortunately, krill do not eat this species. Some lichens and mosses in Antarctica have developed protective pigments against UV radiation. Scientists are researching the effects of increasing UV radiation on other species.

FROZEN FACT

iLLEGAL CFCS
Some countries, such as China, still produce CFC products illegally and sell them on the **black market**. This illegal trade undermines international efforts to solve the ozone problem.

Management of Antarctic issues

The Antarctic Treaty and its follow-up agreements are used to manage Antarctic issues.

THE ANTARCTIC TREATY

In 1959, 12 nations signed the Antarctic Treaty. The treaty sets aside territorial claims, but requires that nations claiming territory look after their areas. The Antarctic Treaty came into force in 1961 and defines Antarctica as the area including Antarctica, the Southern Ocean, and most of the sub-Antarctic islands. The treaty objectives are:

Waste material is sorted at McMurdo base before it is shipped back to the U.S.

* to ban military activities, nuclear weapons testing, and nuclear waste dumping
* to set aside territorial claims
* to promote international scientific cooperation
* to provide freedom of access to all areas
* to conserve the area.

Under the Antarctic Treaty, ships and bases are not allowed to dump garbage, oil, or chemicals into the sea or on land. All waste material must be returned to its country of origin. Ships and bases must have oil spill emergency plans and regular drills. Introduced plants, animals, soil, pesticides, and some plastics are not allowed on Antarctica.

ANTARCTIC TREATY AGREEMENTS

In 1964, an agreement was made to preserve natural areas, plants, and animals in the Antarctic.

CONVENTION FOR THE CONSERVATION OF ANTARCTIC SEALS

This agreement protects southern elephant seals, Ross seals, and some fur seals. Today, seal numbers are recovering and no species are endangered. Seals are no longer hunted commercially in the Antarctic.

CONVENTION FOR THE CONSERVATION OF ANTARCTIC MARINE LIVING RESOURCES (CCAMLR)

❄ The CCAMLR agreement issues licenses and sets catch limits in order to prevent Antarctic species from being overharvested. This ensures that Southern Ocean ecosystems function properly.

❄ CCAMLR controls long-line fishing. It ensures that lines are set at night and weighed down so they sink before seabirds can get the baits.

❄ CCAMLR also started a scheme to identify illegally caught Patagonian toothfish. However, illegal fish are still sold on the black market, further endangering the species.

Scientific information on the feeding patterns of Antarctic animals provides the basis for wildlife management.

The Madrid Protocol protects areas of Antarctica with special values. These are called Antarctic Specially Protected Areas (ASPAs). Scientists must get special permits to do research in these areas.

THE MADRID PROTOCOL

The Madrid Protocol is the main tool used to control human impacts in the Antarctic. The Protocol outlines strict rules to protect the Antarctic. The Protocol also controls human activities, establishes protected areas, and bans mining in Antarctica until 2048.

MONTREAL PROTOCOL

In 1987, the United Nations Environment Program introduced the Montreal Protocol on Substances that Deplete the Ozone Layer. It aimed to limit global CFC production, reducing farther damage to the ozone layer. More than 155 nations have signed the Protocol. Alternative, ozone-friendly products are now mostly used.

THE INTERNATIONAL WHALING COMMISSION (IWC)

In 1982, the IWC stopped all commercial whaling to protect many species from extinction. In 1994, the IWC declared a Southern Ocean Whale Sanctuary in parts of the Antarctic, where no commercial whaling is allowed. This protects whale numbers and maintains Antarctic food chains and ecosystems.

CONSERVATION IN THE ANTARCTIC

There are several other conservation efforts aimed at reducing human impacts in the Antarctic.

WORLD HERITAGE AREAS

World Heritage Areas are areas of such great value that they must be conserved. A World Heritage listing ensures that the area is preserved.

MARINE RESERVES

Australia has large sub-Antarctic marine reserves around Macquarie Island, Heard Island, and McDonald Islands. Armed patrol vessels are used in these areas to protect Patagonian toothfish from poaching. The Auckland Islands Marine Reserve protects the ocean environment from human disturbance.

GREENPEACE

Greenpeace is a non-government conservation organization. Greenpeace built an Antarctic base at Cape Evans and, after staffing it for a year, completely removed it to show that human presence should not damage the environment. Greenpeace played a major role in the IWC's decision to protect whales. The organization supports the Madrid Protocol and continues to draw attention to human impacts in the Antarctic.

The Auckland Islands are protected by a Marine Reserve and are also a World Heritage Area.

The future of the Antarctic

Antarctica holds the secrets to the Earth's past and could help us predict its future. Antarctic issues need to be fully understood and carefully managed. Many people would like to see Antarctica as a World Heritage Area where it would continue to be a model of peace and cooperation for the whole world.

ANTARCTIC CO-OPERATION

Antarctica is a unique place where scientists from all over the world live and work together in a spirit of cooperation in the wilderness. During the International Geophysical Year, from July 1957 until December 1958, scientists cooperated on many research projects. The success of this led to a permanent agreement on Antarctica, the Antarctic Treaty (1961). Scientists are exploring how the continent has changed over time and how it continues to change today and into the future. The results of their shared work may influence the future of the planet.

Scientists from around the world work together in Antarctica.

Glossary

baleen	a bone-like substance found in whales. Plates of baleen hang in the mouths of some whales.
black market	illegal market
bycatch	the animals accidentally caught by fishing nets and lines
endangered	not many left and in danger of becoming extinct
extinction	when a species is no longer living
fossil fuels	coal, oil, and natural gas, which are derived from ancient life forms
fragile	easily damaged
global warming	a global increase in air temperature caused by carbon dioxide released into the atmosphere when we burn fossil fuels such as coal and oil
habitats	the environments where organisms live
heritage	the human tools, buildings, and monuments from the past that are with us today
ice sheet	the thick layer of ice covering most of Antarctica; also called the Antarctic Plateau
ice shelves	layers of floating ice that are still attached to the mainland on three sides
krill	small shrimp-like animals
larvae	the early stage of an insect, crustacean, or fish
long-line fishing	a fishing method that uses baited hooks on miles of lines in the open ocean
Madrid Protocol	an agreement between nations to protect Antarctica from mining
native species	types of plants and animals that grow in a particular area
overfishing	when too many fish are caught in an area and only small numbers are left
phytoplankton	microscopic plant-like algae that form the base of the food chain
pristine	unspoilt and natural
sleds	vehicles on runners, used to pull loads across snow and ice
sub-Antarctic islands	islands surrounding Antarctica
trawling	fishing with nets behind a boat
valley glaciers	slow-moving rivers of ice

Index